Finding Lost Pond

poems by

Pamela A. Mitchell

Finishing Line Press
Georgetown, Kentucky

Finding Lost Pond

ACKNOWLEDGMENTS

I would like to thank the editors of the following journals for their
publication of individual poems:

Intensive Care: More Poetry and Prose by Nurses, 2003, U. of Iowa Press, Iowa
City, Iowa "A Nurse's Farewell"
Knock, 2004, Antioch University, Seattle, WA "For Cassie"
The Healing Muse, 2009, S.U.N.Y. Upstate Medical University, Syracuse, NY
"Excavating Grief"
Pulse: Voices from the heart of medicine, 2010, Change in Healthcare
Publishing, New York, NY. "Redesigning the practice of medicine"
Gyroscope Review, 2018, San Bernardino, C.A, "Grip"
The Trumpeter: Journal of Ecosophy, 2019, Athabasca, Alberta, Canada,
"Nana Log"
Haiku 57, 2019, online, "Heaven"
The Healer's Burden: Poetry and Prose by Professionals, November 2020,
University of Iowa Carver School of Medicine, "Now that I am Surrounded
by Death" new title "Surrounded"

Publisher: Leah Huete de Maines
Editor: Christen Kincaid
Cover Art: Drravenstar Dreamstime.com
Author Photo: Marina Koslow
Cover Design: Elizabeth Maines McCleavy

Table of Contents

In honor of my parents for raising me in a village founded on caring for the sick, and whose lives taught me the power of community and the sanctuary of wilderness.

With gratitude to my siblings for their laughter, loyalty and unwavering support.

For my sons and their wives whose strength, compassion, rootedness in this earth, and choice to live in community while raising my beloved grandchildren, has been my greatest inspiration and joy.

Redesigning the Practice of Medicine

what if we went slowly thoughtfully about the business of healing
what if I bowed   to you and you to me   before we touched aching
bodies
what if we said   out loud   this   is sacred work   might I be made
worthy
what if I blessed your hands and you mine before we began
repairing delivering dressing listening to
broken bodies hungry souls

would we then return to the place where so long ago we felt called
where we knew for sure that we did indeed have hearts
hearts that beat confidently full of ambition
hearts that were courageous enough to break
again and again and again
hearts that were not afraid to weep

at the sheer beauty of fulminating organ
the raw pain of splintered fracture
the howling loss   of bodily movement

what if we were unafraid to weep at the joy of newborns crowning
or the resurrection   of hearts expired

what if we were unafraid to say I do not know the answer
and welcomed Humility into our practice
what if we sat down with Her
and simply   said a blessing

For Cassie

I've sat   outside your door   all morning
guarding you   against yourself   you
cannot promise   staying safe   all morning
I've sat   outside your door   dark
hall   reading
moving   my chair   into
your room   opening curtains
everything shifts   I see
mountains   soft traces   of fog
the light   of day

I watch you sleeping   child of sixteen
arms and chest   wrapped in gauze
covering cuts   you inflicted   razor cuts
I recall   hours ago   listening
your heart   counting its beats
talking with you   telling of tape
I would place   round your breast   arms   legs
hooking wires   watching machine   spit
tracings   of your sixteen-year-old heart

heart already damaged   cocaine's allure
giving you pills   water   easing
withdrawal   asking you breathe
deeply   injecting one then   the other
slender hip
then you wept and I wept
you in pain   and I   at the beauty of
your huge   green eyes

Excavating Grief

Bruce
Eric
Bill
Peter
Rick
David
John
Justin

One long road
stopping here and here and here
pulling into driveways

little pockets of dementia
and Kaposi's
and Cytomegolovirus

blind

where no one knew
except nurses
shoving Subarus into
four-wheel drive
plowing driveways
with prayer

flipping open hatchbacks
revealing baskets
tools—
gauze absorbing dreaded
body fluids   tape
of paper   silk   plastic

securing gauze laying flat
or stretched round skinny
limbs   torso   head

we brought our children
and I know why
we *said*   daycare problems
we *knew* babies' laughter warmed
your hearts

Bruce
Eric
Peter
Rick
Bill
David
John
Justin

We knew your mothers
would not come

We came
dressed your wounds
listened to stories
held you
rocked you

While our babies
toddled round
chasing your puppy

we knew you
loved our babies
Truth be known

we brought them
as angels we held
with one hand

While, you, angel
slipped
right out of the other

Preservation

there are days when the incessant chatter of   mania
or the wails of   depressive disorders   reach   across my desk
toward my solar plexus

my bone marrow cringes   in defense   I move away   gain   distance
I'm sorry I'm leaving soon let me give you   to the next shift
heads lower   shoulders slump   faces frown

for now   my shift is finished

fresh nurses appear   relieve my station   take over my watch
of   hungering souls

I leave   seeking the company of tree frogs   or a child   who
still knows tree frogs intimately   and will tell me about their song
down to the last   detail

A Nurse's Farewell

1.   Calling

My hands guided my nurse's
instinct my hands heard
a million voices howling
yipping like wolf pups
longing for sustenance

My hands listened to stories
of fear and uncertainty
my hands listening drew me forward
magnet pulling me along
Did I sense what lay ahead

2.   Connection

Longing to connect with another
human rhythm to feel a beat
singing within my fingertips

We'd nod in agreement
patient and I slowly
we'd search for the song
that held us in gentle synchrony

3.   Healing

Healing arrived like the flame
I kindled as a child
blowing on a twig singing Rise up flame!
like a bone's fracture line
soon strong enough to bear

the body's weight
like the whisper of a child
propelling my hands toward life
begging to touch the next man
or woman or child with those eyes

God those eyes
that fractured my heart again and again

4.   Pain

Despite hope I know something
deep within me
healing has not stopped by in a long time
instead fear knocks upon the door
fear like the sucking of marrow

from my bones demanding
I be steadfast when my being
silently shatters like safety glass
writhing bodies lash at me
the words of enraged physicians

the voices of those trusted to administrate
threaten to suspend my work
should I become ill one more time
Fear comes with deep fatigue
like being knocked out

the threat the deep fatigue
of witnessing unrelenting sorrow
those with inappropriate diagnosis
those not sick enough sent home to die
and this is how we manage our care

5. Hope

I recall healing's presence
even moments of laughter something
I no longer hear within these walls
except yesterday when laughter slipped in
through the back door by mistake

It's not in my nature as nurse
to let her go

Pain

it is a subterranean place   this   all-encompassing darkness
offering little choice

plunging deeper   to the cold marble   I can only feel   then

my hands become eyes   creatures swim round me   cool to the touch
blue-bloods
backs of scaly silver

within the silent swirling   of wild grasses

my ears open   to the trickle of water   upon stone   when I stand

my breath quickens   swimming deeper   more cold black
marble   deeper   always going deeper

seeking rhythm   I breathe in   and out   waiting

for the next wave

Daughters

Annie

no one to talk to   except Shame
I imagine you   fat ruffles   chubby smiles   so much of me cut
so much of me leaving with you   perform ritual   bury memento
I did
move on   maybe   I never forgave

Elise

years later girl ignites   sound waves bounce   searching   searching
for you
then   no light   no more beating beacon   it is Christmas and there is
no more
light

Elizabeth

one year later   girl ignites   no one prepared   doctor's warning risk
high risk   then
right there while I talk to grandma   you slide out in warm crimson
tide gasping
you are gone   a big piece of me   with you

Chemo

My mother lies quietly
in her hospital bed.

She is saying her rosary
as a nurse inserts the needle.

Gnarled fingers gently grip each bead
while moving slowly toward the next.

She smiles and whispers, *See? Five decades
of this rosary. One for each of you kids.*

She asks if I have given chemotherapy
in all my years of nursing.

I will not tell her how I was excused
from administering those chemicals.

How with each attempt I shook like
autumn leaves rattling in wind.

My mother, however, is strong.
She tells me: *Not to worry, Dolly.*

She wags her finger at me. *God doesn't bring us
this far just to dump us off.*

I am now like the cells of my cancer, she says.
I throw my hands up, shaking my head in confusion.

*Transition, Dolly! I am in transition.
I have transitional cell carcinoma.*

*Now, she continues, let's be still
and honor the Blessed Mother.*

Now That I Am Surrounded By Death

everywhere I look I am encircled

in the last few weeks two of us

laid aside our stethoscopes   and died

another two   are dying still

it is too much   coming home

now my dog   is crying

I suddenly know   it is written everywhere

the scrawl of death's trembling mark

I think of Karla

only next month   she was to fly to China to receive

a baby girl

we heard the code in Emergency

little did we know   it was one of our own

Roommates

My father Nick   is wheeling himself   to his shared
room   in his deaf silence   his blind vision

he gropes   for the hand of his roommate Don   who
is not there   a nurse wheels Nick   to the hospice room

where Don lies   alone   he tells the nurse *I want to go
back with Nick   I want to be   with Nick*

together   they hold hands   these elderly men   veterans
squeezing hands in gentle reminders   back and forth

until   no squeezes

alone   the next day   Nick's right eye
droops   his mouth   puckers   with food

he has forgotten   to swallow   spittle drools
from his now   stroked mouth

word has it   that last week
a nurse   found Don & Nick

side by side   in wheelchairs
gazing   out the window

conversing   in parallel   dementias

Astonished Heart

Leaves me flashing
Surging from my core
Soaking sheets at night

Restlessness triggers like the twitching
Of a marionette's string
My foot jumps
Jumpy legs

Brain contemplates the passing of time
Astonished at the sound of my
Son's voice announcing news
Of pregnancy
His wife's
My daughter
In law

My grandchild-to-be
Now implanting herself
As part of me loosens
And I wonder

Is that what has happened

Since only six weeks prior
A surgeon
Traveled the arteries
Of my heart with
Slender probe announcing
Open. Open. Thirty percent blocked.

Indeed
These are aftershocks I feel
Still warbling within my oldest friend
My body

I tremble at the speed
Of this invasion into my heart

First by surgeon
Then by memories dancing
Through vessels
Hiccoughing enough to
Worry physician who calls while
On vacation

Saying *I'm just not comfortable with this rhythm*
And insists on strapping monitor
To my heart for thirty days
Hoping to capture this renegade rhythm

Which others say must be silenced
Closed up; ablated

My heart knows
It is the full moon's fault

I know those aftershocks are
Always occurring
But cannot always be felt
Unless the heart is open

Therefore force was used
To open and
Navigate

Since this opening
People seem to be jumping in

A man I keep sweeping out day
After day
Who keeps walking right back in
Bald and bold and gentle
Day after day declaring his belief
In this astonished heart of mine

The ducks on my pond who swim by
Laughing lest I become too serious

The neighborhood children who have
Opened a frog nursery in a cardboard box

And now a grandchild gestating
Who saw the opening and hopped
In with the rest

I think how the moon pulls
the ocean
I know it feels the ocean inside
Me
And tugs at my heart opening it
Making more room for more hearts
To jump in

Extra pathways upset the rhythm
Set by the moon who pulls me

And then another surgeon struggling
To evoke the renegade he hopes to ablate
All the while believing I am asleep
But I am not and ask him to stop

I feel an elephant standing on my chest
And he says *just one more try*
But he fails as I sigh relief

And think how often I
Say to those I love
I hold you in my heart

Yearning

for confluence
place of safe harbor

where time
quietly disrobes

standing before
silent moon

her wings unfold
rise soar

silent as Snowy Owl's flight

make sacred space
she cries

and be reminded
who you are

Keeping

Returning from Monhegan I hold
the ocean within me

prisoner now longing
for that desert island

of Solitude

Closing my eyes I recall
the minke whale chasing

herring back and forth
like the rows I knit

of llama yarn and twisted silk

Back and forth she runs
back and forth I pull this yarn

She knits the ocean
into my soul

Ascension
-for Nancy

I.

while following   sea turtles
beneath   shimmering   silverblue

around and   through beds
of coral   watching   listening

snorkels soft   breathing
becomes   silent as

eerie haunting songs
shoot   through water

bounce   off skin
pierce   eardrums

behind masks   of rubber and glass
frightened eyes   swerve

leader nods   points his
thumbs *up   up   go!*

heads nod
fins propel

arms pull
bodies ascend

II.

bouncing hard   upon flat
boats   ascension complete

divers   wait   leader warns
never   have I heard   them this close

sit   do not   raise   paddles
act   of aggression   sit   wait

III.

ocean swells   rises
great   Mother   of the Sea

she   breaches

feast   of the ascension
holy day   of observation

all   eyes   transfix
bodies   freeze

IV.

rising again   she
blows   turns

behind her   another rise
calf   emerges

paddlers   gently   beckon   with soft
tapping   noises   while

leader   whispers   *paddles down! paddles*
down!   do   not   move!

V.

one woman   whispers   *come baby   come!*

magnet   of several   tons
mother   comes   closer

her cool eye   opens   stares
beckons   beckons   pulling all

pulling all   into   the window of
her soul

Nana log

I'm back
in the wild, wet Olympic Forest

how many years gone

how many yet to go

I sit on the bank of the Dungeness
my son ahead casting flies into its peridot flow

his father now gone
gone ahead of us
gone with the years

years he, too, cast in these waters
while I sat listening, watching, recording

now his son, my son, our son waits
for the fly to dip, the trout to bite

our grandson toddling ahead
his hair, his eyes sharply the color
of his papa's
his temperament precisely the strong, shrill, wild
of his papa's

determined, exactly sure of his heart's desire
trout
salmon

all that fights for this life
all that excites the soul

rendering the faith we all long to hold
his father shared, when asked: why not let go?

because, he said with great clarity
it's still good
it's still good

Heaven

Easter vigil candlelight
beside me granddaughter
looks up   smiling

Ode to the Elm Tree

how is it   years ago   most of your kin expired   yet
you survive   flourishing   despite

surgeon   calling you   *nasty elm*   his saw   buzzing
      whacking   releasing   dead limbs   with   thuds

did you   quietly   withdraw   into
      yourself   eventually   birthing   new   leaves

now   in autumn   as earth moves   farther   from   sun
      those leaves   have grown   have   burst

you   cannot   contain   your joy   pop   pop
      pop   bursting hues   singing in   the   color of the Sun

while   beside you   sweet maple   harmonizing

Red Maple

Had I not stepped outside my loneliness
onto this quiet back porch
I'd have missed all your silent
   shouts of glory

Had my neighbor not tended your wounds—
inflicted by beaver's gnawing teeth
I'd have missed all your silent
   shouts of glory

Sanguine sculpture   post
adolescent you reach skyward
leaves silently shivering
   in autumn wind

I vow to sit with you all day
beside your outstretched arms
observing your dance
   of shivering scarlet

I will drink sangria in your honor
we will converse in the ancient
language of trees awaiting the wind
   poised in asana

Grip

pine tree toppled by wind
roots ripped from soil yet
clinging to boulders

I suspect I will grip
when life topples me
tearing my roots

my toes clawing into soil
clutching clumps of earth
my hands grabbing

all that is part of me
all that is dear

When I Leave My Body

Let me rise above the wild roses blooming now
      beside
this river. Let me melt within their scent as it permeates my pores.

Let me descend to iris and cattail conversing within the reeds
      where
mallards hide, scurry and tend their young.

Let the cattails molt from brown to billowing duff; catching breezes
      rising
to be caught in redwing's beak then delivered to nest-in-progress

Let me rise above and savor riparian ways.

Finding Lost Pond

for Peter Hornbeck, master boat-builder

on this crisp autumn day   I am carrying Sweet Pea
upon my shoulder   her paddle   nestled
between thwarts   I lower her   to the stillness
        of this pond

she is small   lightweight   canoe-like   replica
of Adirondack   Lost Pond Boats   used by
fur trappers   portaged   between ponds
        pond hopper

gently grasping gunwales   I slip within her
hold of clear   spun   honey   surrounded now
by water lilies whose umbilical stems   run deep   into
        dark violet water

above me   translucent wings   hum   tiny helicopter
stares   eye to eye   then   buzzing forward
finds its troupe   dragonflies   everywhere
        dragon dance

beside me   loon rises   perfectly painted   fiery red eye
wild   primal   then   eerie chortling cries   wings
flapping   it begins walking   on water
        water bird ballet

from behind a hemlock   Great Blue Heron appears
wings stretch   take flight   skimming pond
never   catching a tip   gliding
        into seamless silence

moving closer to shore   gates of heaven open   more lilies
beaver dam   rising bass   a second heron   takes flight
osprey dives from pine tree   suddenly swoops   snags a bass
        I dip my paddle

then   rest   swirling   into water lilies   dragonflies
nudge me   to floor   of rocking cradle   gazing up
flaming leaves shimmer   in   sanguine golden fire
        a gentle breeze   rises

Pamela A. Mitchell is a nurse who is a native of the Adirondack Mountains of N.Y. where its wilderness was a source of deep sustenance. She attended nursing school at S.U.N.Y. Upstate Medical Center in Syracuse, received her M.F.A. from Goddard College and attended seminary at C.D.S.P. in Berkeley, C.A. She taught writing at S.U.N.Y. Adirondack Community College, Albany Institute of Art, and Saratoga Community Hospital with psychiatric patients. Pamela currently lives in Bend, Oregon where she teaches and consults in geriatric care. When not at work, she can often be found paddling her Hornbeck Boat in the solace of mountain lakes.

CPSIA information can be obtained
at www.ICGtesting.com
Printed in the USA
JSHW042133050421
13300JS00001B/31